IRELAND

Come on our tour of Ireland – its quiet villages and its busy modern cities, its beautiful rivers and fine beaches, its pubs and theatres, castles and towers. Ireland is full of unusual and interesting things to see.

But to understand the Ireland of today, you need to know about Ireland's history too. Who was King Billy, and why is he still important today? What happened on Easter Sunday 1916? Why did so many Irish people leave Ireland in the nineteenth century, and why are so many people coming to Ireland now? Why was the church so important in Ireland, and how is that different today? Take our tour through Ireland's past, and begin to understand Ireland's present.

Henley-in-Arden Site

OXFORD BOOKWORMS LIBRARY

Factfiles

Ireland

Stage 2 (700 headwords)

Factfiles Series Editor: Christine Lindop

TIM VICARY

Ireland

OXFORD UNIVERSITY PRESS

OXFORD
UNIVERSITY PRESS

Great Clarendon Street, Oxford OX2 6DP

Oxford University Press is a department of the University of Oxford.
It furthers the University's objective of excellence in research, scholarship,
and education by publishing worldwide in

Oxford New York

Auckland Cape Town Dar es Salaam Hong Kong Karachi
Kuala Lumpur Madrid Melbourne Mexico City Nairobi
New Delhi Shanghai Taipei Toronto

With offices in

Argentina Austria Brazil Chile Czech Republic France Greece
Guatemala Hungary Italy Japan Poland Portugal Singapore
South Korea Switzerland Thailand Turkey Ukraine Vietnam

OXFORD and OXFORD ENGLISH are registered trade marks of
Oxford University Press in the UK and in certain other countries

© Oxford University Press 2008

The moral rights of the author have been asserted

Database right Oxford University Press (maker)

4 6 8 10 9 7 5 3

ISBN: 978 0 19 423385 9

A complete recording of this Bookworms edition of
Ireland is available on audio CD. ISBN 978 0 19 423386 6

Printed in Hong Kong

Word count (main text): 7120

For more information on the Oxford Bookworms Library,
visit www.oup.com/bookworms

Illustration page 4 by Gareth Riddiford

The publishers would like to thank the following for permission to reproduce images:

4 Corners Images pp 2 Massimo Ripani/SIME, 39 Stefano Amantini; Action Images pp 4 Paul
McErlane/Reuters, 6 FP/NS/Reuters; Axiom pp viii Doug McKinlay, 7 Anna Watson; Alamy p 30 Ros
Drinkwater; Art Archive p 8 Saint Matthew, the Book of Kells, 650-690 AD/Trinity College, Dublin;
Bridgeman Art Library p 19 Sir Edward Carson/The Illustrated London News; Camera Press, London
pp 3 H & D Zielske/Laif, 10 Hartmut Krinitz/Laif, 27 Fulvio Zanettini/Laif, 28 & 29 Wolfgang Fuchs/
Bilderberg, 31 Fulvio Zanettini/Laif, 34 Klaus D. Francke/Bilderberg, 37 (Seamus Heaney) Jason Bell,
38 Wolfgang Fuchs/Bilderberg; Getty pp 18 Michael Nagle, 21 Time & Life Pictures, 22 Walshe/
Hulton; The Illustrated London News p 16; Lonely Planet pp 9 Greg Gawlowski, 33 Chris Mellor;
LP Pictures p 17; Magnum Photos pp 23 Gilles Peress, 25 Stuart Franklin; George Munday p 13;
National Geographic p 1 D.Barnes/Panoramic Images; National Library of Ireland p 14 (siege of
Derry) The Relief of Derry, July 1689 (graphic)/painted by George F.Folingsby/on stone by N.Sarony
and Paul Marny/PD HP (1689)9; Popperfoto p 35; Punchstock p 11; Rex Features pp 14 (Orange
march) John Reardon, 24 (bomb) Sipa Press, 37 (Bono); Scenic Ireland.com p 32 Chris Hall; Werner
Forman Archive p 5 National Museum of Ireland

CONTENTS

Ireland today

1   Ireland's story

There are many different Irelands.

One Ireland is a country with beautiful high mountains, big empty beaches, long deep rivers. People go there to fish and swim and walk. They love Ireland because it is so quiet, and because the Irish people are so nice and friendly.

Another Ireland is a country of stories and music. Most Irish people can sing, and many famous musicians are Irish. A lot of the most famous writers in the English language are Irish too. But some people in Ireland speak only or mostly Irish.

Now look again at Ireland. It is not only a quiet, beautiful, friendly place; it is also a country of blood, bombs, and death. Between 1968 and 1998 thousands of people in Northern Ireland died. But most Irish people are not interested in bombs and guns.

What is Ireland really like? What can you see there? And what happened hundreds of years ago, in Irish history?

Turn the page to begin reading Ireland's story.

2   Around the island

Ireland is an island like a plate: it is higher on the outside than in the centre. Because of this, the centre of Ireland is full of beautiful lakes and rivers, and many people go there to fish and sail. Ireland's largest lake is Lough Neagh. Its longest river, the Shannon, is 260 kilometres long. It goes through many small lakes and two large ones, Lough Ree and Lough Derg.

Most of Ireland's mountains are near the outside of the plate, near the sea. They are not very high – the highest is Carrantouhill (1,040 metres) in the south-west. But they are beautiful, and good places for walks. At the Cliffs of Moher, in the west, you can look 200 metres straight down into the sea. The Giant's Causeway, in the north, is made of strange rocks two metres tall with six sides.

The Giant's Causeway

An Irish lough

There are hundreds of small islands in the sea around Ireland. On the Aran Islands, in the west, most people speak Irish, not English. Life has changed very little here in a hundred years.

Much of the north and west of Ireland is very beautiful. There are hundreds of flowers in the green fields, and there are wonderful beaches and lakes (called 'loughs' in Ireland). The weather is warm and wet, with rain and sun nearly every day. But it is hard to farm here because of the rocks and mountains.

The centre and east of Ireland are very different. The land is good here, and Irish milk and meat are some of the best in the world. Farming is one of the most important jobs in Ireland.

Thousands of horses live here too. Some of the best horses in the world come from Ireland, and Irish people sell

A race in Laytown

horses to Britain, America, Australia, and Japan. People go to watch horse races in many Irish towns, and in Laytown, north of Dublin, there are horse races along the beach every September.

All Ireland's important cities – Dublin, Belfast, Derry, Galway, Limerick, Cork, and Waterford – are near the sea. If we look at Ireland's history, we will see why.

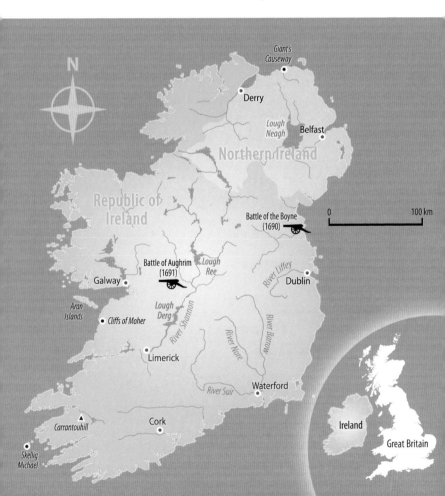

3   Celtic Ireland

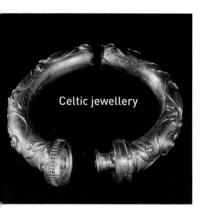

Celtic jewellery

The Irish are a Celtic people. Thousands of years ago, the Celts came to Ireland from western France and northern Spain. They loved singing, and horses, and stories, and they made beautiful gold and silver jewellery. Many men wore gold rings round their necks and arms.

A Greek writer, Diodorus Siculus, wrote this about the Celts:

> The Celts are . . . tall and strong. They wear colourful shirts and trousers. Before they fight they hit their long swords on their shields, and shout with loud voices . . . . They are very good fighters. When a Celt kills a man, he cuts off his head and puts it above the door of his house.

Finn Mac Cool was a famous Celtic fighter. There are many stories about Finn and his men, the Fianna. When he was a boy, he cooked a fish on a fire. This fish knew everything about the world. Finn touched the hot fish with his finger, and put his finger in his mouth. Then he knew everything about the world too. 'I know what is going to happen tomorrow,' he said.

Another famous Celt was Cúchulainn. Cúchulainn's father had a brother called Conor, who was king of Ulster, in the north of Ireland. Conor had a big, dangerous dog which killed many men.

Cúchulainn liked to play a Celtic game called hurling. In hurling, the players can carry a small hard ball in their hands and also hit it with a stick. One day, when Cúchulainn was a boy, Conor called everyone into his house to eat. But Cúchulainn and his friends wanted to finish their game of hurling, so they stayed outside. Conor's dog came out of the house, attacked the young boys and tried to kill them. But Cúchulainn hit the hurling ball into the dog's mouth, and then killed it with his stick. A big fighting dog is called a hound, and so after this, Cúchulainn was called 'The Hound of Ulster.'

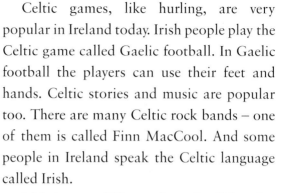

Celtic games, like hurling, are very popular in Ireland today. Irish people play the Celtic game called Gaelic football. In Gaelic football the players can use their feet and hands. Celtic stories and music are popular too. There are many Celtic rock bands – one of them is called Finn MacCool. And some people in Ireland speak the Celtic language called Irish.

Irish is very different from English – for example, the Irish for tree is *crann*, and the word for woman is *bean*. But Celtic people in Wales, Scotland, western France, and northern Spain have languages very like Irish.

A hundred years ago, Irish was nearly a dead language. Most Irish people spoke English, and only the poor people in the west of Ireland spoke Irish. No one taught Irish in schools. Most Irish people speak English today too, but many children learn Irish at school, and many older people in Dublin and Belfast learn it too. They can listen to the Irish language radio station, Raidió na Gaeltachta, and watch Irish language television on TG4. The Irish language is popular again.

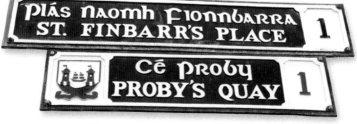

Street names in Irish and English

4 St Patrick, the Church, and the Vikings

In 401 some Irishmen came to Britain. They took many people back to Ireland and sold them. One of these people was Patrick, who was only sixteen. For six years young Patrick worked with sheep on a farm.

Book of Kells

Then, when he was twenty-two, he ran away to France. He learned about God from monks at a school in a French monastery. In 432 he went back to Ireland to teach the Irish about God. The Irish kings listened to him, and he built an important church in Armagh.

A hundred years later, Ireland was one of the most important Christian countries in Europe, with beautiful churches and monasteries everywhere. Irish writers wrote famous, important books like the *Book of Kells*, which you can see in Dublin today, and there are pictures of St Patrick in many Irish churches.

Another Irish churchman, called Brendan, sailed to Scotland, Iceland, Greenland, and America in a small

A round tower

leather boat. Some people said that this was not possible, but in 1976 an Englishman, Tim Severin, built a leather boat called *Brendan* and sailed it from Ireland to Iceland and America. You can see the *Brendan* at Craggaunowen in County Clare in the west of Ireland.

There were many beautiful, expensive things in the Irish churches and monasteries, and Norwegian Vikings came to Ireland to steal them and kill the monks. Because of this, the monks built tall round towers beside their monasteries. When the Vikings came the monks ran into the towers to hide. You can see these towers in Irish villages today.

One of the most interesting Irish monasteries is on Skellig Michael. It is an island in the Atlantic sixteen kilometres south-west of Ireland. It is a beautiful, windy place. The island is 240 metres high, and in bad weather no boats can get there. 'There is no danger here,' the Irish monks thought; but they were wrong. In 824, Vikings came in their long ships to attack Skellig Michael too.

But some Vikings came to Ireland to stay. They built towns by the sea – Dublin, Cork, Waterford, and Limerick.

The Celts liked to live in the country, but the Vikings lived in towns. Some of the Vikings married Celts, and learned the Celtic language.

The Vikings came to the north of Ireland too. One day two different Viking ships came to a beautiful place in Ulster. Both groups of Vikings wanted to stay there and build a town, but there were too many of them. The two groups of Vikings looked at each other angrily.

'We must fight,' said a Viking from the first ship. 'The winners will live and keep the land, and the losers will die.'

'No,' said a man from the second ship. 'I have a better idea. Let's race to the beach in our ships. The first man who holds the land in his hand can keep it. His people can stay, and the others must leave.'

So the two ships raced towards the beach. One man stood at the front of each ship, ready to jump down to the beach. Then one ship went in front of the other. The man in the first ship looked back at the second

ship, and laughed. 'We're going to win,' he said. 'This land will belong to us.'

'No, it won't,' said the man in the second ship angrily. 'You will never win. Never!' Suddenly, he took out his sword, and cut off his hand with it. Then he threw the hand over the heads of the men in the first ship. The hand fell on the beach, and its bloody fingers closed on the land.

'This is our land,' said the man with one hand. 'It will never belong to you. Never, never, never!'

That is the story of the Red Hand of Ulster. You can see the Red Hand on the flags of Northern Ireland. To learn why it is so important, we need to learn a little more about Irish history.

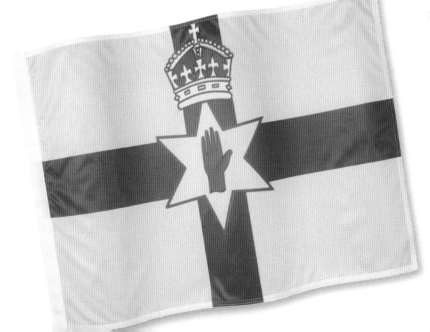

5   The English come to Ireland

A thousand years ago, Ireland had many kings and they often fought each other. In 1152 one Irish king, Dermot MacMurrough, attacked another Irish king, Tiernan O'Rourke, and took his wife. Tiernan O'Rourke was the friend of a third king, Rory O'Connor. In 1166 Rory O'Connor was made king of all Ireland. At this time, Tiernan and Rory attacked Dermot MacMurrough, but Dermot escaped to England.

Dermot then asked the king of England, Henry the Second, to help him to fight Rory and Tiernan. So in 1169 Henry's men came to Ireland and fought Rory and Tiernan, but they did not go home again. They took more and more of the land for themselves. They built cities by the sea, and big castles. Henry called himself King of England and Ireland. But not all the Irish were happy about this.

For the next four hundred years, English kings tried to rule Ireland from Dublin. But it was very difficult. The Irish did not listen to the King of England – he was too far away.

In 1536 the English church changed from Catholic to Protestant. So England was a Protestant country, but Ireland was still Catholic. For the Protestant English, their

One of Henry's castles

king was the most important man in the Church, but for the Catholic Irish, the most important man was the Pope – the leader of the Catholic Church – in Rome. There was a lot of fighting in Ireland about this, and usually the English won. The kings of England took more land from the Catholic Irish, and gave it to Protestant Englishmen and Scotsmen. This plan was called the Plantation of Ulster, because much of the land was in Ulster, in the north of Ireland. Englishmen from London built a new town in a place called Derry, and called it Londonderry.

The Catholic Irish were angry about this and wanted their land back. In 1641 the Catholics attacked the Protestants in Ulster. They took their houses and clothes and killed thousands of people.

Eight years later, in 1649, Oliver Cromwell took an English army to Ireland. Cromwell was the leader of the English after the death of King Charles the First. The English soldiers killed thousands of Catholics in a town called Drogheda.

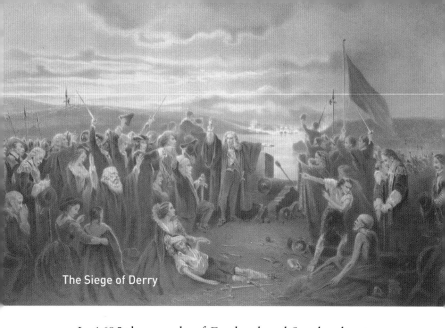
The Siege of Derry

In 1685 the people of England and Scotland got a new king – James the Second. He was a Catholic, and he was not very popular. Many people wanted a different king, and in 1688 William of Orange, a Dutch Protestant, came to England. He was married to James's daughter Mary, and he wanted to be king of England, Scotland, and Ireland.

In those three countries people who wanted James to be king fought against people who wanted William to be king. Most of James's friends were Catholics in Ireland. With his help, they tried to get their land back again. They got most of it, but they could not get Londonderry. When they attacked it, the Protestants ran inside the city walls and closed

An Orange march

the gates. For 105 days, the Catholic soldiers tried to get inside and kill them. The Protestants were cold and afraid and hungry. They ate cats and dogs and horses, but they did not open the gates. 15,000 people died during this time, which was called the Siege of Derry.

At last, three Protestant ships came to Londonderry with food and soldiers, and the siege was over. After that the new Protestant English King, William of Orange, won two very important battles against the Catholics: the Battle of the Boyne in 1690, and the Battle of Aughrim in 1691. The Catholic Irish didn't fight a big battle again for 100 years.

So for the next hundred years life was very difficult for the Catholic Irish. Keeping their land or going to Catholic schools or Catholic churches was very difficult and they could not speak or vote in Parliament. All the important people in Ireland were Protestants, and all the big, beautiful houses and the best farms belonged to Protestants.

In most countries, people read about history in books; in Ireland, history is alive today. Every year, Protestants in Londonderry march to remember 1688. In Belfast, on 12 July, Protestant Orangemen march with music and songs about King William of Orange – often called 'King Billy'– and the Battle of the Boyne. Every year, Catholics are angry about these marches.

6   The Great Hunger

In 1795 and 1798 the Irish, with the help of French ships and soldiers, fought the British. But the British won, and many Irishmen – mostly Catholics – were killed. Three years later, in 1801, the Act of Union made Ireland and Britain one country, with one Parliament, in London. For a hundred years after this, Catholic Irishmen (called Nationalists) wanted to change the Act of Union, and Protestants (called Unionists) wanted to keep it.

At this time, in the west of Ireland, many poor Catholics lived on very small farms. They had very little money, and often they had only potatoes to eat. The poor, stony land was not good for many things, but it was good for potatoes. But in the 1840s something killed the potatoes. One day they were fine, and then suddenly they were black and dead. The poor Irish farmers and their families had nothing to eat. Thousands of them died, and many more went on ships to America, to find a new and better life.

Looking
for potatoes

Some rich Protestants were happy when the poor farmers started to leave. They wanted to keep cows on their land, so they asked the ships to take the poor people away from Ireland to America. But hundreds of people died on the ships too.

When the Irish people came to America, they lived in big cities, like New York. Every year on St Patrick's Day thousands of Americans march through New York, and remember how Irish people died, because there was no food. It is the biggest St Patrick's Day parade in the world, because so many Irish people live in America.

When these poor Irish people died, the Irish language nearly died with them. Most Catholic churchmen spoke English, and the government told Irish teachers to use English in school. Only poor people spoke Irish. 'Irish is

Leaving Ireland

St Patrick's Day Parade, New York

not important,' the teachers and churchmen said. They thought that speaking English was more modern.

But some people thought that this was wrong. In 1893 a group of Irish writers tried to help the Irish language. 'Irish is the language of the Irish people,' they said. 'Many countries have a language, games, music, and stories that belong to them. We must have those things too.'

A lot of people agreed with them. These people called themselves Sinn Fein, which is Irish for 'We Ourselves.' At first, the people in Sinn Fein were only interested in Irish language, music, and games. But later, they began to think about other things too.

'We don't want to belong to Britain,' they said. 'We want Ireland to be a free country.'

7   Fighting to be free

By 1900, life was a little better for Catholics in Ireland. They could have land, they could vote and speak in Parliament, they had Catholic schools and churches. But most Catholics were very poor, and every year, thousands of them went to America or Britain to look for work.

Catholic Irish Nationalists wanted to end the Act of Union. They wanted an Irish Parliament to decide about things in Ireland. But the Protestants did not want to give it to them – and, not for the first time, they were ready to fight for the things that they wanted.

Sir Edward Carson
with the Protestant army

In 1914, the British government decided to give Ireland an Irish Parliament. 'Ireland will still belong to Britain,' they said. 'But the Irish Parliament will decide on Irish things, like Irish schools, roads, and police.' Most Irish Nationalists were happy about this, but the Protestant Unionists were angry.

Most Protestants lived in Northern Ireland near Belfast. This part of Ireland is called Ulster. Soon the Protestant Unionist army began marching through the streets of Belfast with their leader, Sir Edward Carson. They wanted to keep the Act of Union. 'Ulster will fight,' they said, 'and Ulster will be right!'

The British government did not know what to do. They wanted to give Ireland a Parliament, but they did not want to fight the Unionists. But then, in 1914, the First World War started. Most of the Protestant Unionists, and many thousands of Irish Catholics, went with the British army to fight against Germany.

But many Irish Nationalists stayed in Ireland. 'We don't want to fight the Germans,' they said. 'We want the British to leave Ireland. Perhaps the Germans can help us.'

In 1916, a group of Irish Nationalists – mostly Catholics – decided to fight for a free Ireland. They were interested in Irish music, Irish history, the Irish language, and Irish games. But now they bought guns in Germany and tried to bring them to Ireland in a German ship. Their leader, Patrick Pearse, wanted much more than an Irish Parliament. He wanted Ireland to be free from Britain.

On Easter Monday 1916, Pearse and his men went into the Post Office, in the middle of Dublin. Pearse walked to the door. 'Irishmen and Irishwomen,' he said. 'Ireland belongs to the Irish people! Today Ireland is a free country!'

But the British did not agree. For six long days there was a battle in Dublin, and many men died. After the battle, the government said that Pearse and fourteen other important men had to die, and they died in prison. Nearly two thousand other Sinn Fein men went to prison.

Easter Monday 1916 was a very important day in Irish history. After that day, everything was different. In his poem *Easter 1916* the Irish writer William Butler Yeats wrote:

> *All changed, changed utterly.*
> *A terrible beauty is born.*

The Dublin Post Office, 1916

The Irish Republican Army

In 1919, Sinn Fein started to fight the British again. The Sinn Fein army was called the Irish Republican Army, or IRA. From 1919 to 1921 the IRA killed hundreds of policemen and soldiers, and the police and soldiers killed hundreds of IRA men too. In Dublin, there were IRA men and women everywhere, but it was very hard for the British soldiers to find them. The IRA leader was Michael Collins, but the British government didn't even have a photo of him!

In 1921 the British government decided to talk to Sinn Fein and the IRA, and in that year, for the first time in history, most of Ireland had an Irish government, with an Irish President in Dublin.

But the Irish Republic is only three-quarters of Ireland. One quarter, in Northern Ireland, stayed British. And here, fifty years later, the trouble between Protestants and Catholics started again.

8   Northern Ireland

In 1921, about 60 per cent of the people of Northern Ireland were Protestant, and about 40 per cent were Catholic. Today the numbers are about 53 per cent and 40 per cent. Most of the Protestants want to be British, and most of the Catholics want to be Irish. Hundreds of people have died because of this.

From 1921 to 1971 Northern Ireland had a Parliament at Stormont. There were always more Protestants than Catholics, so the Protestants could do what they wanted. Protestants had most of the best jobs and the best houses. Most of the police were Protestant too, and they were afraid of the IRA. At the same time, many Catholics were afraid of the police. Sometimes the IRA tried to kill the police, and the police hit back at the Catholics. It was a circle without an end.

In 1968 Catholics started to ask for a better life. They marched through the streets of Belfast and Derry, asking for better jobs and houses. But the Protestant police

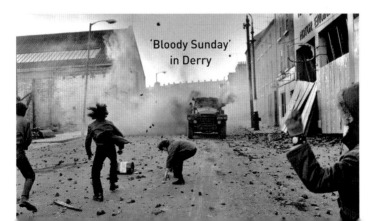

'Bloody Sunday' in Derry

After a bomb

and Orangemen attacked the Catholic marchers. Many marchers were badly hurt, and all of them were angry and afraid.

In 1969 British soldiers came to Northern Ireland to try to stop the fighting, and at first many Catholics were happy to see them. But then the IRA started to kill soldiers and policemen, and so the British soldiers and police tried to find the IRA and put them in prison. Sometimes they put the wrong people in prison, and so the Catholics didn't like the British soldiers.

Over the next thirty years, many terrible things happened. On 'Bloody Sunday' – 30 January 1972 – British soldiers killed 14 Catholic marchers in Derry. 'The marchers had guns,' the soldiers said. But nobody found any guns. On 'Bloody Friday' – 21 July 1972 – the IRA put 22 bombs in Belfast, all at the same time. 9 people died and 130 people were hurt, Protestant and Catholic, British and Irish. Some of them lost arms and legs.

The IRA put bombs in pubs and streets and shops. They killed soldiers and policemen, but they also killed thousands of ordinary people. Protestants in the Ulster Defence Association – the UDA – killed thousands of ordinary Catholics too. These Protestant fighters are called Loyalists.

By 1979 there were hundreds of IRA and UDA men in prison. At first they were political prisoners, like soldiers

An IRA wall painting, Belfast

in prison during a war. They could wear ordinary clothes, and they did not do prison work. Then Margaret Thatcher, the British Prime Minister, decided that this must stop. 'These men are criminals,' she said, 'so they must be the same as other prisoners.'

Because of this some prisoners decided in 1980 to stop eating. They drank water but they did not eat. Day after day, they got thinner and thinner. After 66 days, the first man, Bobby Sands, died. Then another man died, and another. Ten men died in prison, because they wanted to be political prisoners. Most British people thought Mrs Thatcher was right, but a lot of Irish Catholics didn't agree. More and more of them started to vote for Sinn Fein.

In many parts of Northern Ireland there are Nationalist or Loyalist paintings on the walls of houses. The Loyalists usually show the Red Hand of Ulster, or King William of Orange and the Battle of the Boyne. The Nationalists show Celtic pictures, and pictures of Bobby Sands. Both of them often show men with guns.

In 1998, the British and Irish governments met with Sinn Fein and the Ulster Unionists. They wanted to end the fighting in Northern Ireland. Together, they made the Good Friday Agreement. This Agreement said that Catholics and Protestants must work together in the government of Northern Ireland.

Today, Catholics and Protestants still do not agree about many things in Northern Ireland. But after thirty years of fighting, people are starting to talk to each other. And most people are happy about that.

9 Dublin and Belfast

Dublin Dublin is the most important city in the Republic of Ireland. Its population (the number of people who live there) is 496,000. The River Liffey goes through the centre of Dublin. Some people say that Ireland's famous black beer, Guinness, is water from the River Liffey, but it is not true. But you can walk beside the river, and drink Guinness in a pub when you are thirsty.

One of the most beautiful buildings beside the river is the Custom House. There is a nice walk along the river from the Custom House to the O'Connell Bridge. North of the bridge is O'Connell Street. Here you can see the Post Office, famous for Easter Monday 1916. Not far from here is St Mary's, Dublin's biggest Catholic church.

The Custom House

South of O'Connell Bridge is Trinity College, Ireland's oldest and most famous university. In here you can see Ireland's oldest books, like the *Book of Kells*, which is a thousand years old. The beautiful Bank of Ireland is opposite Trinity College. Ireland's first Parliament was in this building.

Near Trinity College you can see the famous statue of Molly Malone. People say that she was a poor but beautiful girl, who sold fish called cockles and mussels on the streets to make money. But sadly, she died when she was still young. There is a famous Irish song about Molly:

> *In Dublin's fair city*
> *Where the girls are so pretty*
> *I first set my eyes on sweet Molly Malone*
> *As she wheeled her wheelbarrow*
> *Down streets broad and narrow*
> *Singing 'Cockles, and mussels, alive alive-oh!'*

Molly Malone

Music in a Dublin pub

Some of Ireland's best town houses are in Merrion Square. Many of Ireland's most famous writers, soldiers, and leaders lived here. They walked and talked in the small park in the square, or in St Stephen's Green, not far away. Between Merrion Square and St Stephen's Green is Leinster House, the home of Ireland's Parliament today.

Dublin also has Phoenix Park, one of the largest parks in Europe. Ireland's President lives here, in a house called, in Irish, Áras an Uachtaráin. Not far away from the Phoenix Park is the old Kilmainham Prison. Here visitors can see how some of Ireland's most famous men and women lived in prison.

Dublin is a city of theatres, music, and fine shops too. And there are dozens of pubs, big and small. Many people like to go to the pub to drink beer, talk, and tell stories. For example, there is a story about a visitor and an Irish farmer in the country. 'Excuse me, can you tell me the way to Dublin, please?' the visitor asks. The farmer thinks for a long time. Then he says: 'No, I'm sorry. If you want to go to Dublin, this is the wrong place to start.'

Belfast
Belfast (population 276,000) is the biggest city in Northern Ireland, famous for the ships, aeroplanes,

McHugh's Bar

and clothes that were made here. The *Titanic* was built here in the Harland and Wolff shipyard. In 1912 the *Titanic* was the biggest, fastest, most expensive ship in the world. 'This ship can never sink,' people said. But when the *Titanic* went to sea for the first time, it sank, and about 1,500 people died. Many of them were poor Irish people who wanted to start a new life in America. Now this part of the city is called the Titanic Quarter, and it has new shops, offices, bars, cafés, and hotels. But you can still see the big Harland and Wolff cranes, called Samson and Goliath, from all over Belfast.

At Victoria Square, in the centre of Belfast, there are new shops, restaurants, and cinemas. And there are fine old buildings to see – City Hall, the Custom House with its wonderful statues, the Ulster Bank, and McHugh's Bar – the oldest building in Belfast. Once it was a house by the Belfast River, and today it is a modern bar.

10 Four Irish cities

Cork Cork is the second largest city in the Republic of Ireland. In 820 the Vikings attacked a Christian monastery here, and then stayed to build a town by the River Lee. Cork is in the south-west of Ireland and it has a wonderful harbour for ships. Many poor Irish people sailed from Cork to America at the time of the Great Hunger, and today ships and planes go from Cork all over the world.

123,000 people live here today, and the city of Cork is famous for music, dancing, theatre, and film. Many visitors come here too, on their way to the beautiful south-west of Ireland. In 2005 Cork was the European Capital of Culture.

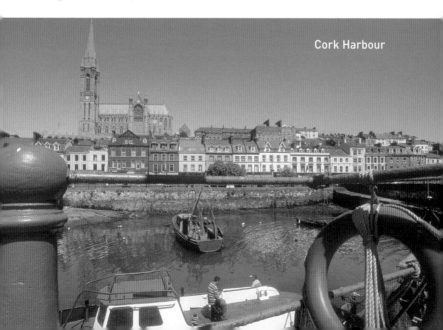

Cork Harbour

Londonderry, or Derry

Derry, with a population of 105,000, is the second city of Northern Ireland. Protestants call it Londonderry, because in 1600 English Protestants from London built a city here, but Catholics call the city Derry. There was a small monastery here, beside the River Foyle, in the time of the Vikings, but the great walls of Londonderry were built in the 1600s. You can walk around these walls today: they are one and a half kilometres long and nearly six metres wide. The old guns from the Siege of Derry are still there on the walls.

But many people want to forget the battles of the past. In the last week of October, thousands of people come to Derry for the Halloween festival. There is music, theatre, and a big parade, in the biggest street party in Ireland.

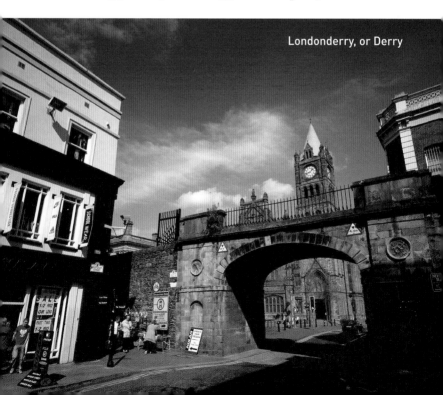

Londonderry, or Derry

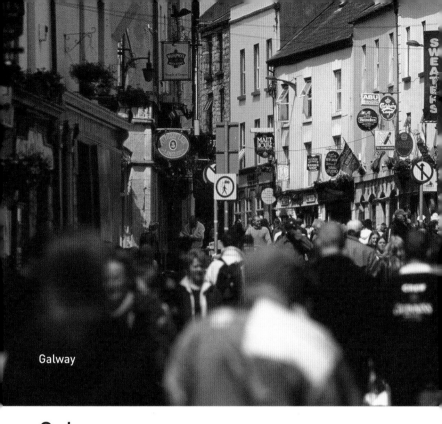

Galway

Galway

Galway (population 65,800) is in the west of Ireland, at the mouth of the River Corrib. In this part of the country the Irish language is very strong, and you will see it and hear it everywhere. It is a centre for Irish music, singing and dance, and there is an Irish language theatre in Galway too.

From Galway you can visit Connemara, with its beautiful wild lakes and mountains. The Aran Islands are close by too. People speak Irish here, and many visitors like to come to these wild, lonely islands to hear Irish music in the pubs and see the difficult life of the islanders.

Waterford

Waterford (population 45,000) is in the south-east of Ireland. It was Ireland's first city; the

Vikings came here in the 850s, and they came back in 914 to make the city. It is famous for its glass (people have made glass here since 1783) and for the ships that were built here. Three rivers meet the sea at Waterford – the Rivers Barrow, Nore and Suir – and there are fine mountains and beaches to visit in this part of Ireland.

Waterford

11 Stories, music, and dancing

Irish people love stories, and many great writers were born in Ireland. Jonathan Swift (1667–1745) was a churchman in Dublin. In his book *Gulliver's Travels* a man called Gulliver visits many strange countries. In Lilliput all the people are about ten centimetres high and in the country of the Houyhnhnms horses are cleverer than people. But when Gulliver comes home, nobody believes his stories.

James Joyce (1882–1941) wrote all his stories about Dublin. His most famous book, *Ulysses*, is 700 pages long. It is the story of everything that one man, Leopold Bloom, does in Dublin in one day – 16 June 1904. And every year on 16 June – 'Bloomsday' – people visit Dublin to talk about *Ulysses* and to visit the places in the story.

Joyce's friend, Samuel Beckett (1906–89) won the Nobel Prize for his work in the theatre. His most famous work, *Waiting for Godot*, is about two poor Irish men who are waiting for a man called Godot. Perhaps Godot is a man, perhaps he is God – they don't know. But he never comes.

Joyce and Beckett were born in Ireland, but they went to work and live in France. They had new and exciting ideas, and some people in Ireland did not like them. To the Irish government and the Catholic Church, books like *Ulysses* were wrong, and after 1929 Irish people could not buy books like these in the shops. Life was difficult in other ways too – many people had large families and little money. Ireland was a poor country, and it was difficult to find work. Every year, many young people left Ireland to look for work in other countries.

Because of these things some singers too were very angry about life in Ireland. Bob Geldof was born in Ireland in 1951. His mother died when he was seven, and his father was often away from home, so young Bob was often alone. He saw many poor people in Dublin, and his band, the Boomtown Rats, sang loud, angry songs. In their song *Banana Republic*, they said Ireland was a poor country with a bad government, and too many police and churchmen:

> *Everywhere I go now*
> *And everywhere I see*
> *The black and blue uniforms*
> *Police and priests*

Bob Geldof wanted to change the world, and in 1985 he planned some concerts called Band Aid and Live Aid. He used the money from the concerts to help hungry people in Africa. In 2005 he did this again, with a concert called Live 8. With another Irish musician called Bono, Bob Geldof asked the presidents of many countries to give help to Africa.

Bono

Bono is from an Irish group called U2. Some people say that U2 are the biggest rock band in the world. Like Bob Geldof, the band do a lot of work to help the poor people of the world. Two other famous Irish pop groups are the boy bands Boyzone and Westlife. There are famous women singers too, like Sinead O'Connor, Enya, and Aoife Ní Fhearraigh.

There are many famous singers and writers from Northern Ireland too. Seamus Heaney was born in 1939 on a farm near Derry. In 1995 he won the Nobel Prize for his poems, and people read them all over the world. The famous singer Van Morrison grew up in Belfast in the 1950s.

Seamus Heaney

Most people in Ireland love music. People sing in pubs in every Irish town, and Irish songs are very popular on television in other countries. Ireland has won the Eurovision Song Contest for the best pop song in Europe seven times; this is more than any other country.

The Irish word for party is *céili* – a time for people to play music, tell stories, and dance. For hundreds of years, the Irish people have loved dancing at ceilis. In the 1700s, dancing teachers went from town to town. People lived in small houses, so they often danced on the country roads. They wore their best clothes to dance, and played music all day and all night.

In many Irish dances, the dancers keep their hands still by their sides, and move their feet and legs very quickly. Today thousands of Irish children learn Irish dancing, and the best dancers from all over the world come to dance in Ireland too. The Irish dancers Michael Flatley and Jean Butler are famous in many countries – thousands of people have seen them in *Riverdance* and *Lord of the Dance*.

Irish dancers

12

A country for young people

Today, many things are changing in Ireland. It is a country of young people: nearly 50 per cent of its people are under twenty-five. Fifty years ago, the Catholic church was full of old men, and they decided what people could do. Life was difficult for women and young people. Today, the church is important, but the ideas of women and young people are important too. Two of Ireland's presidents were women – Mary Robinson and Mary McAleese. For Ireland's young people the future is about pop music and computers as well as farming and horses.

Ireland is a part of the European Union, and most Irish people are very happy about this. Ireland is not a poor country any more; a lot of business people come to Ireland and build factories. Now, perhaps 10 per cent of Ireland's population are people who have come from other countries to find work there. Many come from Poland and other countries in Eastern Europe, and others come from China and countries in Africa. Today, young Irish people do not have to leave their country to find work; they can find work at home. Ireland is an interesting, exciting place for young people.

But of course, there are always problems. There is more crime in Ireland than before. And in Northern Ireland, the problems are not over. Every year the Protestant Unionists march through the streets with their music. 'We will always be British,' they say, and they sing about William of Orange. 'The British must leave Ireland,' say the Catholic Nationalists in Sinn Fein. The Unionists and the Nationalists cannot both have what they want. Here, history helps no one.

But most Irish people, in the north and south of Ireland, do not want bombs, guns, and fighting. They want to enjoy life. They want people to visit their island, to walk in their beautiful mountains, fish in their quiet rivers, drink and sing and laugh in their pubs, dance at their ceilis, and most important of all, to talk. Most of the time, the Irish are the friendliest people in Europe. And the three most important words in the Irish language are:

> *Céad míle fáilte*
> 'A hundred thousand welcomes.'

GLOSSARY

attack   to try to hurt or kill someone

battle   a fight between armies in a war

beer   a strong, brown-coloured alcoholic drink

bomb   a thing that explodes and damages people or things

Catholic   a member of the Christian church that follows the Pope in Rome

Christian   following the teachings of Jesus Christ

crane   a big machine that lifts heavy things

destroy   when something is destroyed, it is dead and finished (e.g. fire destroys a forest)

farm   (*n & v*) land and buildings where people grow things to eat and keep animals for food; **farmer** (*n*)

game   something that you play that has rules, e.g. football, tennis

God   the 'person' who made the world and controls all things

government   a group of people who control a country

history   all the things that happened in the past

idea   a new thought or plan; a picture in your head

king   the most important man in a country

kiss   to touch something with your lips

land   a piece of ground

leader   someone who is the most important person in a group, a government, etc

leather   the skin of an animal that is used to make things like shoes and bags

monastery   a place where monks live, work and pray

monk   a religious man who lives with other religious men in a monastery

musician   a person who makes music

Nobel Prize   one of six international prizes given each year for excellent work in literature, medicine etc

ordinary   not strange or special

parade   a line of people who are walking together for a special reason, while other people watch them

Parliament   the people who make the laws in a country

poem   a piece of writing, often with short lines, showing feelings or ideas

popular   if something is popular, a lot of people like it

president   the leader of a country that does not have a king or queen

problem   something difficult to understand, or find an answer for

Protestant   a person who believes in the Christian God and who is not a Catholic

pub   a place where people go to have a drink, meet friends, etc.

republic   a country where the people choose the government and the leader

Republican   (in Northern Ireland) a person who believes that Northern Ireland should be part of the Republic of Ireland

rule   (of a king or queen) to control a country

Saint   part of the name of a holy person, often written as St

shield   a big piece of wood or metal that soldiers carry in front of their bodies when fighting

sink   to go down under water

surrender   to stop fighting because you cannot win

sword   a long sharp knife for fighting

throw   to use your hand to send something quickly through the air

university   a place where people go to study after they leave school

Viking   one of a group of people from Scandinavia who attacked countries in northwest Europe in the 8th to 11th centuries

vote *(v)*   to choose someone in an election by marking a piece of paper

war   fighting between armies of different countries

welcome   you say this to a visitor to show that you are happy to see them

Ireland

ACTIVITIES

ACTIVITIES

Before Reading

1 Which of these things or people do you think you are going to find in a book about Ireland? Tick seven boxes.

☐ wine   ☐ potatoes
☐ dancing   ☐ skyscrapers
☐ beer   ☐ pubs
☐ hot dogs   ☐ basketball
☐ apples   ☐ horses
☐ elephants   ☐ George Washington
☐ Bob Geldof   ☐ Vikings
☐ fish and chips   ☐ hotels

2 Read the back cover of the book, and the introduction on the first page. How much do you know now about Ireland? Are these sentences true (T) or false (F)?

1 There has been peace in Ireland for a long time.

2 Something important happened on Easter Sunday 1916.

3 Ireland is a hot, dry country.

4 Many Irish people left the country in the seventeenth century.

5 To understand Ireland today you need to look at its past.

6 Singing and dancing are important in Ireland.

ACTIVITIES

While Reading

Read Chapters 1, 2, and 3. Circle the correct word.

1 Most Irish people can *ski/sing*.

2 Most of Ireland's *mountains/lakes* are near the sea.

3 The Giant's Causeway is made of strange *islands/rocks*.

4 Life on the Aran Islands changes *quickly/slowly*.

5 In the north and west of Ireland it is *warm and wet/dry and hot*.

6 Irish *wine/milk* and meat are some of the best in the world.

7 Irish people sell *dogs/horses* to many countries.

8 Many Celtic people wore gold rings around their *necks and arms/feet and legs*.

9 Hurling is a popular Celtic *game/dance*.

10 Irish is very *like/different from* English.

Read Chapter 4 and then put these sentences in the correct order.

1 _____ One ship went in front of the other.

2 _____ The bloody fingers of the hand closed on the land.

3 _____ They decided to race to the beach in their ships.

4 _____ Then a man in the second ship cut off his hand.

5 _____ The man with one hand said, 'This is our land.'

6 _____ Two groups of Vikings wanted to build a town in the same place in Ulster.

7 _____ He threw it over the first ship to the beach.

8 _____ 'We're going to win,' said a man in the first ship.

Read Chapter 5. Choose the best question word for these questions, and then answer them.

What / When / Who / Why

1 _____ was king of Ireland after 1169?
2 _____ was the Plantation of Ulster?
3 _____ brought an English army to Ireland in 1649?
4 _____ did the Siege of Derry end?
5 _____ won the Battle of the Boyne and the Battle of Aughrim?
6 _____ do Protestants march on 12 July?

Read Chapters 6, 7, and 8, and then answer the questions.

1 What big change happened in Ireland in 1801?
2 What happened to many poor Irish people in the 1840s?
3 Why do people march in New York on St Patrick's Day?
4 Why did the group called Sinn Fein begin?
5 Why did the Protestants make an army in 1914?
6 What happened in Dublin on Easter Monday, 1916?
7 When did the Irish government begin to meet in Dublin?
8 What happened on 'Bloody Sunday'?
9 Why did ten people die in prison in 1980?
10 What is the Good Friday Agreement, and who made it?

Read Chapters 9 and 10. Then match the places with the things you will find there.

1 O'Connell Street
2 Trinity College
3 The Harland and Wolff shipyard
4 The Custom House, Belfast
5 Cork

6 Londonderry

7 Galway

8 Connemara

9 Waterford

a The *Book of Kells*

b wild lakes and mountains

c the River Lee

d an Irish language theatre

e the cranes called Samson and Goliath

f glass factories

g wide walls 400 years old

h the Post Office

i wonderful statues

Read Chapters 11 and 12 and decide if the sentences are true (T) or false (F). Change the false sentences into true ones.

1 Jonathan Swift was a churchman in Londonderry.

2 Samuel Beckett won the Nobel Prize for his work in the church.

3 After 1929 you could not buy *Ulysses* in Ireland.

4 Bono is a famous Irish musician with a group called V2.

5 Seamus Heaney was born in Northern Ireland.

6 Ireland has won the Eurovision Song Contest ten times.

7 More than half of Irish people are under twenty-five.

8 Ireland has had two woman presidents called Mary.

9 Ireland wants to join the European Union.

10 A lot of business people come to Ireland and build factories.

ACTIVITIES

After Reading

1 **Match the sentences with the people. Then use the sentences to write a short description of each person. Use pronouns (*he, she*) and linking words (*and, but, so, when, who*).**

Bob Geldof / James Joyce / Molly Malone / Patrick Pearse / Saint Patrick / William of Orange

1 _____ was a poor but beautiful girl.

2 _____ was angry about the lives of poor people.

3 _____ was the leader of the Irish Nationalists.

4 _____ is called 'King Billy' by Protestant Orangemen.

5 _____ was born in 1882.

6 _____ learned about God in a French monastery.

7 _____ took men to the Post Office on Easter Monday, 1916.

8 _____ wrote a book about one day in Dublin.

9 _____ became King of Ireland after James the Second.

10 _____ sold cockles and mussels on the streets of Dublin.

11 _____ wanted to change the world.

12 _____ came back to Ireland to teach the Irish about God.

13 _____ won the Battle of the Boyne against the Catholics.

14 _____ made Ireland an important Christian country.

15 _____ left Ireland and went to live in France.

16 _____ died when she was young.

17 _____ died in Kilmainham Prison in Dublin.

18 _____ planned some big concerts which made money for people in Africa.

2 Use the clues below to complete this crossword with words
   from the story. Then find the hidden place name in the
   crossword.

					1						
				2							
	3										
		4									
			5								
	6										
7											
			8								
		9									
		10									
11											

 1 Patrick Pearse was this for the Irish Nationalists.
 2 These people lived a quiet life on Skellig Michael.
 3 To stop fighting because you cannot win.
 4 A piece of ground.
 5 The Orangemen belong to this religion.
 6 These visitors to Ireland built cities like Dublin and Cork.
 7 The Irish one lives in a house in Phoenix Park, Dublin.
 8 Guinness is a famous black kind of this.
 9 There is one of these on St Patrick's Day in New York.
10 Land where people grow food and keep animals.
11 All the things that happened in the past.

 The hidden place name is _____.

3 Etsuko visited Dublin for the weekend and sent you this postcard. Circle the correct words.

Hello/Goodbye from Dublin

I *arrived/left* here on Friday and walked along the *river/sea* through the centre of town. I stopped at a *pub/college* and drank some of Ireland's famous *beer/tea* called Guinness. It was *brown/black* and very strong! I *saw/looked* at the Post *Office/Bridge*, which is famous for Easter *Sunday/Monday*, 1916. Then I visited *Christchurch/Trinity* College to *see/watch* Ireland's oldest *book/statue*, which is a *hundred/thousand* years old. It was very beautiful. And just near there I took a photo of the statue of Molly *Malone/Patrick Pearse* selling *cheese/fish* from her wheelbarrow.

Tomorrow I am going to visit the *prison/house* of Ireland's *King/President* and walk in one of the *biggest/smallest* parks in *Europe/America*. Dublin is a wonderful *city/country*!

See you soon.
Etsuko

4 Complete this report about Celts and Vikings in Ireland, using the words below (one word for each gap).

ago, attack, built, came, different, English, fighters, first, found, games, jewellery, language, monasteries, north, Norway, Spain, speak, stole, Ulster, Wales, Waterford

Both the Celts and the Vikings _____ to Ireland from other countries – the Celts from France and _____, the

Vikings from _____. Both were strong _____, but the Celts also made beautiful _____.

The Celts arrived _____, thousands of years _____ . They brought with them Celtic _____, like hurling, and also music. The Irish _____, which some people still _____ in Ireland today, is Celtic too, but it is very _____ from _____. There are other Celtic languages in _____, Scotland, and parts of Europe.

The Vikings began to _____ Ireland around 800. Often they attacked the _____ and _____ the beautiful things that they _____ there. But some Vikings stayed and _____ towns. _____, Dublin and Cork were all Viking towns. They also went to live in the _____ of Ireland in _____.

5 Choose a city or part of Ireland that you would like to visit. Find some more information about it, and make a poster or give a talk to your class. Look for answers to these questions:

What do you know about its history, famous people, or famous places?
What do people make or do in this part of Ireland?
What can visitors see or do there?
Why would you like to go there?

You can find more information about places to visit in Ireland at www.tourismireland.com.

ABOUT THE AUTHOR

Tim Vicary is an experienced teacher and writer. He is married with two children and lives in the country in Yorkshire, in the north of England. He often goes to Ireland on holiday, and particularly likes visiting the ring of Kerry in the south-west of Ireland. He has written two historical novels about Ireland, *The Blood Upon the Rose* and *Cat and Mouse*, and teaches a university course on Northern Ireland. He also enjoys horse racing and keeps and rides horses of his own. He has recently published a crime novel called *A Game of Proof* under the name Megan Stark.

He has written or retold more than fifteen stories for Oxford Bookworms, from Starter to Stage 3. His other Oxford Bookworms titles at Stage 2 are *Death in the Freezer* (Crime and Mystery) and *Grace Darling* (True Stories).

OXFORD BOOKWORMS LIBRARY

*Classics • Crime & Mystery • Factfiles • Fantasy & Horror
Human Interest • Playscripts • Thriller & Adventure
True Stories • World Stories*

The OXFORD BOOKWORMS LIBRARY provides enjoyable reading in English, with a wide range of classic and modern fiction, non-fiction, and plays. It includes original and adapted texts in seven carefully graded language stages, which take learners from beginner to advanced level. An overview is given on the next pages.

All Stage 1 titles are available as audio recordings, as well as over eighty other titles from Starter to Stage 6. All Starters and many titles at Stages 1 to 4 are specially recommended for younger learners. Every Bookworm is illustrated, and Starters and Factfiles have full-colour illustrations.

The OXFORD BOOKWORMS LIBRARY also offers extensive support. Each book contains an introduction to the story, notes about the author, a glossary, and activities. Additional resources include tests and worksheets, and answers for these and for the activities in the books. There is advice on running a class library, using audio recordings, and the many ways of using Oxford Bookworms in reading programmes. Resource materials are available on the website <www.oup.com/bookworms>.

The *Oxford Bookworms Collection* is a series for advanced learners. It consists of volumes of short stories by well-known authors, both classic and modern. Texts are not abridged or adapted in any way, but carefully selected to be accessible to the advanced student.

You can find details and a full list of titles in the *Oxford Bookworms Library Catalogue* and *Oxford English Language Teaching Catalogues*, and on the website <www.oup.com/bookworms>.

THE OXFORD BOOKWORMS LIBRARY
GRADING AND SAMPLE EXTRACTS

STARTER • 250 HEADWORDS
present simple – present continuous – imperative –
can/cannot, must – going to (future) – simple gerunds …

Her phone is ringing – but where is it?

Sally gets out of bed and looks in her bag. No phone.
She looks under the bed. No phone. Then she looks behind
the door. There is her phone. Sally picks up her phone and
answers it. ***Sally's Phone***

STAGE 1 • 400 HEADWORDS
… past simple – coordination with *and*, *but*, *or* –
subordination with *before*, *after*, *when*, *because*, *so* …

I knew him in Persia. He was a famous builder and I
worked with him there. For a time I was his friend, but
not for long. When he came to Paris, I came after him –
I wanted to watch him. He was a very clever, very dangerous
man. ***The Phantom of the Opera***

STAGE 2 • 700 HEADWORDS
… present perfect – *will* (future) – *(don't) have to, must not, could* –
comparison of adjectives – simple *if* clauses – past continuous –
tag questions – *ask/tell* + infinitive …

While I was writing these words in my diary, I decided
what to do. I must try to escape. I shall try to get down the
wall outside. The window is high above the ground, but
I have to try. I shall take some of the gold with me – if I
escape, perhaps it will be helpful later. ***Dracula***

STAGE 3 • 1000 HEADWORDS
… should, may – present perfect continuous – *used to* – past perfect
– causative – relative clauses – indirect statements …

Of course, it was most important that no one should see Colin, Mary, or Dickon entering the secret garden. So Colin gave orders to the gardeners that they must all keep away from that part of the garden in future. *The Secret Garden*

STAGE 4 • 1400 HEADWORDS
… past perfect continuous – passive (simple forms) –
would conditional clauses – indirect questions –
relatives with *where/when* – gerunds after prepositions/phrases …

I was glad. Now Hyde could not show his face to the world again. If he did, every honest man in London would be proud to report him to the police. *Dr Jekyll and Mr Hyde*

STAGE 5 • 1800 HEADWORDS
… future continuous – future perfect –
passive (modals, continuous forms) –
would have conditional clauses – modals + perfect infinitive …

If he had spoken Estella's name, I would have hit him. I was so angry with him, and so depressed about my future, that I could not eat the breakfast. Instead I went straight to the old house.
Great Expectations

STAGE 6 • 2500 HEADWORDS
… passive (infinitives, gerunds) – advanced modal meanings –
clauses of concession, condition

When I stepped up to the piano, I was confident. It was as if I knew that the prodigy side of me really did exist. And when I started to play, I was so caught up in how lovely I looked that I didn't worry how I would sound. *The Joy Luck Club*

BOOKWORMS · FACTFILES · STAGE 2

Seasons and Celebrations

JACKIE MAGUIRE

In English-speaking countries around the world people celebrate Easter, Valentine's Day, Christmas, and other special days. Some celebrations are new, like Remembrance Day and Mother's Day; others, like the summer solstice, go back thousands of years.

What happens on these special days? What do people eat, where do they go, what do they do? Why is there a special day for eating pancakes? Who is the 'guy' that children take onto the streets in November? And where do many people like to spend the shortest night of the year in England? Come on a journey through a year of celebrations, from New Year's Eve to Christmas.

BOOKWORMS · FACTFILES · STAGE 2

Rainforests

ROWENA AKINYEMI

Deep rivers, tall trees, strange animals, beautiful flowers – this is the rainforest. Burning trees, thick smoke, new roads and cities, dead animals, people without homes – this is the rainforest too. To some people the rainforests mean beautiful places that you can visit; to others they mean trees that they can cut down and sell.

Between 1950 and 2000 half of the world's rainforests disappeared. While you read these words, somewhere in the world people are cutting down rainforest trees. What are these wonderful places that we call rainforests – and is it too late to save them?